Healthy children's lunches

Healthy children's lunches

52 brilliant little ideas for junk-free meals kids will love

Mandy Francis

brilliantideas

CAREFUL NOW

Follow the tips in this book and you should find that you're able to reduce the amount of junk food your children eat at lunch time while still giving them food they love. Never put your child on a diet and if you're worried about his or her weight or are thinking of radically changing his or her diet you should consult a doctor. Good luck and happy cooking.

Infinite Ideas would like to thank Sally Brown, Kate Cook and Mandy Francis for their contributions to this book.

First published in 2007 by
The Infinite Ideas Company Limited
36 St Giles
Oxford, OX1 3LD
United Kingdom
www.infideas.com

A CIP catalogue record for this book is available from the British Library

ISBN 978-1-905940-10-3

Designed and typeset by Baseline Arts Ltd, Oxford
Printed in Singapore

Brilliant ideas

Introduction 10

1. **Lunchbox makeover**.................12
Now you've decided that you'd like your children to eat healthy packed lunches here are a few practical tips to get you started.

2. **What's wrong with sugary foods?**14
It's easier to cut back on excess sugar in your family's diet than you might think.

3. **Shake off the salt** 16
How much salt do they really need?

4. **Vitamins and minerals** 18
You could be forgiven for thinking that some of those packaged foods aimed at kids are healthy.

5. **It's 'reduced' so it must be ok, right?** 20
Wrong – let's see what those 'reduced' claims on the label really mean.

6. **You say 'flavour' – I say 'flavoured'** 22
How can you tell whether the flavour comes from something real or is just synthetic?

7. **Lite bites**..................................24
Do you really know what those low fat label claims mean?

8. **The way to 5 a day**...................26
How can you get your vegetable-phobic children to eat their greens?

9. **E-asy does it** 28
Do you sometimes think you need to take a chemistry exam to understand food packaging?

10. **What do they need?** 32
Confused about what your child should be eating when he starts school? Look no further.

11. **Gourmet sandwiches**..............34
These don't just have to be a piece of cheese or ham slapped in between two slices of bread. Read on...

12. **Feeling fruity**..........................36
Children should ideally eat at least two portions of fruit a day, since they're packed with valuable nutrients and fibre.

13. **Healthy pre-teens**...................38
Find out what your 7–10 year olds need.

14. **The basics**..............................40
The building blocks of the ideal packed lunch.

15. **Leave it out**...........................42
Here's a run down of the worst things you can put in your child's lunch.

16. **Use your loaf**..........................44
Brown, white, wholemeal, granary, multigrain, pitta or ciabatta - which bread is best for your child?

17. **Weighty issues**.......................46
If you're worried your child may be overweight read on.

18. **Get the right fat-itude**............48
All children need some fat in their diets, but it has to be the right kind.

19. **Chicken little**..........................52
Chicken can vary enormously in taste and texture, depending on the quality of bird that you buy.

20. **Pasta la vista baby**.................54
Pasta is a good source of carbohydrate for your children's lunches.

21. **Fat ideas**.................................56
Here are a few ideas to help you keep fats at a healthy level.

22. **Rice is nice**.............................58
Kids will love this versatile food.

23. **Vegging out**............................60
Basic nutrition know-how to help if your child's just turned veggie.

24. **High or low?**...........................62
How do you know whether a product you're buying is high or low in fat?

25. **Spuds they'll like** 64
A handy, filling food packed with energy-boosting carbohydrates – potatoes are the main ingredient for a host of quick-to-make dishes children will love.

26. **Fishing for compliments** 66
There are shoals of tasty fish varieties out there just waiting to be turned into healthy, child-friendly meals.

27. **Meaty issues** 68
Red meat has had a bad press over the last few years but don't rule it out of your child's diet. It's a great source of important nutrients.

28. **Anything with a pulse**.............72
Don't dismiss pulses as vegetarian fodder.

29. **Cheese please**..........................74
Tempt your kids away from those processed, stringy cheese sticks with a little imagination.

30. **Egg them on** 76
Eggs are a good source of protein and a brilliant stand-by for a quick, healthy lunch.

31. **Chocs away**............................78
Consistently voted the number one favourite food by children, even the healthiest diet has to find room for a little chocolate now and again.

32. **Just desserts**..........................80
A healthy diet doesn't mean pudding has to be off the menu.

33. **Whizz it up** 82
Smoothies and shakes really are a great way to bump up your child's daily fruit intake.

34. **Little chefs** 84
Teaching your children to cook is one of the very best ways to encourage them to adopt healthy eating habits.

35. **Bursting with health**...............86
Boost your family's immune systems with the right diet and lifestyle habits to fight off some of the worst infections.

36. **Supersavers** 88
Feeding your children healthily needn't be expensive if you follow these tips.

37. **Save more** 92
Here are some more tips on keeping the weekly food bill down.

38. **Salt solutions** 94
How can you minimise the amount of salt your children eat?

39. **The big freeze** 96
If you make a few lunchbox favourites and keep them in the freezer you won't spend all of your evenings making up packed lunches.

40. **Big kids** 98
How to encourage hungry teens to eat nutritious meals.

41. **Calcium is key** 100
All children need an adequate intake of calcium, to help with bone and dental health.

42. **Iron out deficiencies** 102
Make sure your kids aren't missing out on this essential mineral.

43. **I think I'm going to be sick** ... 104
The good news is, many children do eventually go on to outgrow their food allergies and intolerances.

44. **Snack attack** 106
Make sure what they eat for morning break is healthy too.

45. **Fruit machine** 108
Hit the jackpot with these exciting alternatives to apples, pears and bananas.

46. **Start right** 112
Many schools run breakfast clubs – and if you drop your child off early in the morning for one of these you'll need to provide something substantial for him to eat.

47. **Sugar, sugar** 114
Whilst the odd bag of sweets will not do any harm it's important to cut down on your family's everyday consumption of sugar.

48. **A big problem?** 116
What to do if you think your child is overweight.

49. **Plan-it organic** 118
The best food you can buy for your family – or just a big con?

50. **Eat fat** 120
When is fat good for your kids?

51. **Happy shoppers**......................122
Healthy eating starts with the
shopping trip.

52. **Petits gourmets**.....................124
Challenge your child's palate with
some unusual foods and flavours.

Introduction

Have you been making nothing but processed cheese sandwiches for the last few weeks? Do you always end up packing your little angel off to school with crisps and chocolate bars because you're worried she won't eat anything else? You are not alone. If you've run out of lunch box ideas – or simply don't know where to start – this little book will give you the inspiration you're looking for.

A well-balanced packed lunch will provide your child with all the energy and nutrients she needs for a busy day at school or nursery. But according to a recent survey of children's lunch boxes, carried out by the Food Standards Agency, the contents of most packed lunches are way too high in saturated fats, sugar and salt. The same survey also showed that almost of half of the lunch boxes examined did not contain fruit and that most of the lunches included heavily processed snacks, crisps, chocolate, biscuits and sugary fizzy drinks.

Whilst it's tempting to include junk food 'treats' in your child's lunch box – or processed foods that have been heavily advertised on TV – don't. A meal that's poor in nutrients and high in salt, sugar and fat will sap your child's energy levels and mental alertness – and over time could even set the foundations for future health problems and obesity.

So if you're now at a loss as to what to give your child, don't worry – it really is quite simple to put together a healthy packed lunch. The next 52 chapters will give you plenty of ideas, recipes, hints and tips so that you can send your children, whether they're 5 or 15, off to school with balanced lunch packs. It's not all about deprivation (there are plentry of 'treats' recipes) and although most of the ideas involve more effort than throwing a few packets into your child's school bag you don't need to be a top-flight chef to create them.

The key is variety – and perseverance. Your children may rebel initially, especially if all their friends are bringing cheese strings and fizzy pop to school. If they turn their noses up at something don't give up straight away, just try one of the other ideas in this book – you may even come up with a few recipes of your own.

1. Lunchbox makeover

Now you've decided that you'd like your children to eat healthy packed lunches here are a few practical tips to get you started.

1. Make a shopping list and don't take the children shopping with you. If the children come with you they'll spend the time trying to persuade you to buy all their favourite junk foods, giving you less space to think and making it harder for you to remember all the healthy things you need to buy.

2. Don't give your children pocket money. It sounds harsh but surveys show that lunch and pocket money tends to get spent on sweets or junk food. If your child wants something specific such as a toy or CD tell them you'll put aside a certain amount a week for them until they've saved up the full amount.

3. Make the lunch box fun and functional. Put dips and salads in brightly coloured pots, cut sandwiches into interesting shapes with cookie cutters and wrap them in coloured bags sealed with stickers. Make sure your child's lunch box is going to be kept cool and check that it won't spend all morning somewhere hot (like on a radiator).

Here's an idea for you

Buy insulated lunch bags. There is a wide variety available (often featuring the latest cartoon or toy sensation); or try the Hungry Jungle range of brightly coloured packs featuring cartoon animals – available in John Lewis and from online retailers. If you're organised, make the lunch the night before and store it in the fridge so everything is thoroughly chilled by morning. Alternatively freeze a carton of juice and add it to the lunchbag just before your child leaves the house. It will kep food cool and be defrosted and ready to drink by lunchtime.

2. What's wrong with sugary foods?

It's easier to cut back on excess sugar in your family's diet than you might think.

Sugars occur naturally in many foods such as fruit and milk – which is fine, we don't need to worry about those. The sugar that is of concern is added sugar, the stuff in fizzy drinks, sweets, biscuits, some breakfast cereals and jam.

Foods that contain a lot of added sugar tend to have quite a high calorie content and low levels of nutrients. Sugary foods also don't tend to fill children up – the rapid rise and dip in blood sugar that sugary foods can cause means children will often want another sugary snack soon after having the first one. Sugary foods and drinks can also cause tooth decay, particularly if they are eaten or drunk between meals. This includes fruit juice and honey.

Here's an idea for you

Instead of fizzy drinks and juice drinks with added sugar, go for water or unsweetened fruit juice (for young children these should be diluted 50:50 with water). If your child likes fizzy drinks then try diluting fruit juice with sparkling water. Alternatively get hold of natural fruit concentrates, in flavours such as pear, apple and blackcurrant, and dilute these with still or fizzy water. You can find them in heath food shops, including Holland and Barrett.

3. Shake off the salt

How much salt do they really need?

Our bodies need a very small amount of salt to work properly. Eating too much salt can raise blood pressure. And people with high blood pressure who eat too much salt are three times more likely to develop heart disease or have a stroke than people with normal blood pressure. If children have too much salt now, it may well affect their health in the future. It is also likely to give them a taste for salty food, which means they're more likely to continue eating too much salt when they grow up.

Below are the recommended maximum amounts of salt children should have in a day, although it's better if they have even less than these amounts

- 1 to 3 years – 2g a day (0.8g sodium)
- 4 to 6 years – 3g a day (1.2g sodium)
- 7 to 10 years – 5g a day (2g sodium)
- 11 and over – 6g a day (2.5g sodium)

6g of salt is approximately a teaspoonful – so you can see the tiny amount your child really needs. When looking at labels on foods it's helpful to know that 0.5g sodium/100g indicates that the food is high in sodium.

Here's an idea for you

If you're determined to reduce your child's salt intake then one obvious thing to remove from his lunchbox is that packet of crisps. However, you're going to have to come up with a replacement if you're to avoid tantrums. Try popcorn instead – it's very easy to make and children will have fun helping. First melt a small amount of butter in a deep pan with a heavy lid. Once it's melted add enough popcorn kernels to just cover the base of the pan and put the lid on. (You'll need to hold the lid on or you'll have a kitchen covered in popcorn.) After a few minutes you'll start to hear the corn popping quite vigorously. Once the pops have become very spaced out it should be safe to remove the lid. Leave to cool before putting in the lunchbox. If plain popcorn is 'boring' try flavouring with melted honey and cinnamon.

4. Vitamins and minerals

You could be forgiven for thinking that some of those packaged foods aimed at kids are healthy.

Manufacturers love to boast how many vitamins and minerals their products contain but this can sometimes be a smokescreen for their products' less desirable ingredients.

Whatever the product says on the front, always take a look at the nutrition box on the back. A 500ml blackcurrant drink that claims to be 'rich in vitamin C' can also contain a whopping 14 teaspoons of sugar – the equivalent of three and a half packs of chewy sweets. A pot of fromage frais that claims to be 'a source of calcium' may also contain up to 4 teaspoons of sugar. A teaspoon of sugar is approximately 4g.

'Added calcium' is another claim flashed across the packets of some children's processed cheese snacks. Added calcium there may be – but many of these snacks contain extremely high levels of salt – and a clutch of additives too if you look at the nutrition box on the back.

Here's an idea for you

Regular cheese is rich in calcium without the addition of questionable chemicals. Go on a taste test with your children – most supermarket deli counters will let you sample several cheeses so go at a quiet time of day and let them choose what cheese to buy that week. A good real alternative to stringy cheese would be mozzarella (the soft balls of cheese that come packaged in liquid rather than the pressed type you slice from a block). Mozzarella has a similar fun-to-eat texture. In place of cheese spread, triangles or cheese dips try Quark, half fat mascarpone or flavoured cottage cheese. Processed cheese slices can be replaced with slices of Cheddar, Leerdammer, Emmental or Edam. It's also much cheaper to buy cheese this way than in portion-sized packages. Only give small portions because all cheese is relatively high in fat and salt.

5. It's 'reduced' so it must be ok, right?

Wrong – let's see what those 'reduced' claims on the label really mean.

The term 'reduced' sugar, salt or fat can be confusing. To be able to claim a product has 'reduced' levels of anything means the food has to contain 25% less of the nutrient referred to than was in the original product. Unfortunately, if that particular product was very high in sugar, salt or fat in the first place – the 'reduced' version may still contain very high levels of sugar, salt or fat.

For example, some 'reduced fat' packets of crisps actually have more fat grams than other, regular packets of crisps – because their original version was particularly high in fat. Ditto a 'reduced sugar' soft drink may still have a high sugar content, because the amount of sugar in it was through the ceiling in the first place.

If your kids are used to having a chocolate bar in their lunch boxes they're not going to take its disappearance lying down. Ease them in with a small piece of chocolate refrigerator cake – not exactly a health food but at least you can control what goes into it.

Here's an idea for you

Chocolate refrigerator cake.

All children will love pounding the biscuits for this simple, no-cook recipe. Line a 1lb loaf tin with lightly greased foil. Place 350g/12 oz digestive biscuits (this also works well with Ginger Nuts) in a plastic bag and bash with a rolling pin until you have a bag of small pieces and crumbs. Tip the crumbs and 50g/2oz dried fruit (raisins and chopped apricots, pears or dates work well) into a mixing bowl. Melt 110g/4oz plain chocolate, 110g/4oz butter and 1 rounded tablespoon of golden syrup in a pan or microwave – then stir into the dry ingredients until all crumbs are coated with chocolate. Tip the mixture into the lined tin and press down firmly with the back of a spoon. Refrigerate overnight, before turning out, removing the foil and slicing.

6. You say 'flavour' – I say 'flavoured'

How can you tell whether the flavour comes from something real or is just synthetic?

Believe it or not, there is a big difference between flavour and falvoured when it comes to food labelling. A strawberry 'flavour' yogurt is one that has been made to taste like strawberries through the use of artificial flavours – it doesn't have to contain any fruit at all. A strawberry 'flavoured' yogurt on the other hand has most of it's flavour coming from real strawberries. If you're not sure, buy one that says it contains real fruit. All of these could contain high quantities of sugar though so the best option is to make your own.

Here's an idea for you

Make your own yogurts. Don't worry – we're not suggesting you start fermenting cultures in the corner of your kitchen. All you need to do is go out and buy a large pot of natural, unsweetened yogurt. (Bio yogurt is even better since it contains some of the 'friendly bacteria', good for digestive health.) Either chop up soft fruits such as strawberries, raspberries or blueberries and sweeten with a little honey or, if your children don't like lumps of fruit in their yogurts, puree or mash the fruits and stir them in. This should also colour the yogurt a reasuringly lurid shade of pink or purple. Make sure you invest in some small pots with leak-proof lids or you'll end up with some awfully messy lunch boxes.

7. Lite bites

Do you really know what those low fat label claims mean?

'Light' or 'lite' on a package can be used to refer to the texture of a product as well as the amount of fat it does or doesn't contain – there's no real legislation for these two terms as yet. So a fluffy, high fat chocolate mousse could still be labelled as 'light'. X% fat free can also be misleading and although the food industry is supposed to have dropped this label, many foods still advertise themselves as 97% fat free, 90% fat free and so on. If you see something like a packet of biscuits or dessert labelled as 97% fat free don't assume it will be better for your family, or lower in calories. Although it may contain just 3% fat it may be packed with sugar. Manufacturers often add sugar to replace fat they've cut out. This will increase the calorie content of the product and if the body can't use all the calories it obtains from the food for fuel, it will store them as fat. So read the label carefully.

Here's an idea for you

If you cook these delicious crisps yourself you'll know exactly how much fat is going into them. Because the crisps are cooked in the oven they need very little oil and using other root vegetables instead of potatoes also helps your children towards their '5 a day'. Even so they should be an occasional treat rather than an everyday feature of your child's lunch. Sweet potato, parsnips, uncooked beetroot and swede make unusual (and slightly sweet) vegetable crisps. Slice the vegetables thinly using a potato peeler, toss in a little oil (you really don't need much to coat them), and lay out – without overlapping – on a baking tray. Bake in a pre-heated oven at 190°C/375°F/gas mark 5 for 20 minutes, then flip your crisps over and bake for a further 10–15 minutes until cooked. Once cool put a handful in a bag or small pot as part of a packed lunch.

8. The way to 5 a day

How can you get your vegetable-phobic children to eat their greens?

- Don't make compromises. Only buy and serve the foods that you want your child to eat.
- Eat vegetables yourself to set the right example.
- Try fun and colourful raw veg such as carrot batons, baby sweetcorn, and sweet red pepper strips.
- Offer brightly coloured alternatives to 'greens' such as sweetcorn, peppers, sweet potatoes and swede. Use them to garnish a dish and make it look more exciting.
- Try to find a good role model. If you know of a child who eats up their greens, invite them to tea and lavish praise on their eating habits in front of your child.
- Keep the dessert well out of sight until the main course is finished.
- Don't give too much attention to your child when he says he won't eat something. Instead, reinforce the positive by commenting when he does eat the right foods.

And if all the above fails? Resort to stealth tactics. Hide those veggies in casseroles, stews and pasta sauces by pureeing a handful or two of steamed veg and simply stirring it in to your child's favourite food.

Here's an idea for you

Chocolate courgette cake

If your child really refuses to eat anything remotely vegetable like try this recipe – great for putting in lunch boxes. It may not be the healthiest way to encourage her to eat her greens – but hey – it's a start! Line a 20 x 35cm baking tray with baking paper and preheat the oven to 190°C/350°F/gas mark 5. Beat together 125g/ 4½ oz softened butter, 125ml/ 4½ fl oz sunflower oil, 1 tsp vanilla extract, 200g/7oz soft brown sugar and 100g/3½ oz caster sugar until fluffy. Gradually add 3 eggs, beating well after each one and then 125ml/ 4½ fl oz milk until mixed thoroughly. Fold 350g/12oz plain flour, 2 tsp baking powder and 4 tbsps cocoa into the mixture. Stir in 450g/1lb peeled and grated courgettes and pour the mixture into the tin. Bake for 35–45 minutes until cooked through – leave to cool in the tin.

9. E-asy does it

Do you sometimes think you need to take a chemistry exam to understand food packaging?

EU legislation requires most additives used in foods to be labelled clearly in the list of ingredients, either by their name or by their E number. A survey into conventional processed children's foods undertaken by organic food company Baby Organix discovered that most foods contained an average of five additives (ingredients that you wouldn't add if you were making it yourself). The biggest culprits were children's desserts, cereal bars, breakfast cereals, children's drinks and frozen beef burgers.

Forewarned is forearmed however. If you're concerned about E numbers and don't recognise many of the ingredients in the food you are thinking of buying don't buy it. Azo dyes are colourings found in many foods but there is evidence that some can trigger asthma, skin rashes, rhinitis (a runny nose) and may even be responsible for hyperactivity in some children, although this is hotly contended by many manufacturers. The E numbers for food colourings run from E100–E180. Preservatives are there to prolong shelf life but some can trigger side effects in children with asthma. Skin rashes and gastrointestinal problems can also be linked to some preservatives. E numbers for preservatives run from E200 to E285.

Here's an idea for you

Once you've read the labels of a few of your kids' favourite foods you'll probably wonder what is safe to give them. However, manufacturers are becoming more aware of parents' concerns and so you should be able to find alternatives without the nasties in. Lyme Regis Foods make a range of fruit and cereal bars aimed at kids which are free of artificial flavours, colours and preservatives. They even do a range featuring Disney characters – making them very attractive to children – and are available in branches of Asda, Tesco, Sainsbury's, Waitrose and Holland & Barrett.

'Variety's the very spice of life, that gives it all its flavour'

WILLIAM COWPER, writer and poet

10. What do they need?

Confused about what your child should be eating when he starts school? Look no further.

In one day the average 5–6 year old will need:

- **6 servings** of starchy carbohydrates (bread, potatoes,rice, pasta, breakfast cereals).
  1 serving is: 1/2 a slice of bread *or* 1/3 cup of cooked rice or pasta *or* 1/2 cup breakfast cereal *or* 2 small potato pieces.
- **2 servings** of fruit
  1 serving is: 1/2 an average pear, apple *or* orange *or* 1/4 cup tinned or cooked fruit *or* 1/3 cup 100% fruit juice
- **3 servings** of vegetables
  1 serving is: 1/4 cup cooked vegetables *or* 1/2 cup salad.
- **2 servings** of dairy (milk, cheese, yogurts, fromage frais etc)
  1 serving is: 1/2 cup of milk or a small pot of yogurt *or* a matchbox-sized piece of cheese.
- **2 servings** of meat, poultry, fish, eggs, pulses, nuts and seeds
  1 serving is: 30g of meat, fish or poultry *or* one egg *or* 1/3 cup cooked pulses *or* 20g nuts.

Fats and sweets should be kept to an absolute minimum.

Here's an idea for you

Every little helps so try to get some vegetables into your child's lunchbox. Try colourful vegetable crudités. Chop carrots and celery into small batons, cut red, yellow or orange peppers into thin strips and put in some mini sweetcorn. Present the vegetables in colourful pots or bags and give your kids something interesting to dip the veg into such as guacamole (page 49), hummous (page 73) or low fat soft cheese. If your child brings his lunch home saying that he doesn't like it, take the offending food away without comment – but don't give up. Try it again a couple of days later. Experts reckon you should expect to offer an unfamiliar food at least eight to ten times before a child will accept it.

11. Gourmet sandwiches

These don't just have to be a piece of cheese or ham slapped in between two slices of bread. Read on...

- Always use butter or spread on bread, and take it right to the edges of the bread. That way there'll be a waterproof seal to stop the filling making the sandwiches soggy.
- Pack any salad garnishes such as tomato and cucumber slices or lettuce separately. Salad tends to go flabby and make the sandwiches soggy very quickly. Make 'one filling' sandwiches and provide a selection of veggies that can be eaten on the side with fingers instead – such as carrot, baby sweetcorn, cucumber and celery batons, cherry tomatoes etc.
- Ring the changes with wraps, pitta bread, bagels, foccacia and rolls.
- Sandwiches should be carefully wrapped in greaseproof paper or foil so they keep their shape, then packed snugly in an airtight box so they don't get squashed in transit.

Here's an idea for you

Tuna, sweetcorn and red pepper pitta

This colourful sandwich will provide a portion of protein and go towards a serving of vegetables. Mix half a small can of tuna, a few spoons of sweetcorn and ¼ of a chopped red pepper with a little mayonnaise. Lightly toast a pitta bread, cut in two and fill each pocket with half the tuna mixture.

Cream cheese and date bagel

Bagels are lower in fat than other breads and the dates in this filling make it a good sandwich if your child has a sweet tooth. Slice the bagel in half and toast it. Allow it to cool before spreading on low fat cream cheese. Chop up two or three dates and sprinkle them over the cheese before sandwiching the two halves back together.

12. Feeling fruity

Children should ideally eat at least two portions of fruit a day since they're packed with valuable nutrients and fibre.

If you're having trouble getting your youngsters to eat enough fruit there are several simple steps you can take to encourage them.

- Always buy the very best quality fruit you can afford. Look for organic and choose home-grown whenever possible since home-grown fruit will have been picked most recently.
- Ensure that whatever fresh fruit you choose to give your child is well and truly ripe. A ripe, juicy pear is delicious – a hard, not-quite-ready-to-eat one could put your child off pears for years.
- Don't stick to just two or three fruit favourites. Broaden your family's fruit repertoire for maximum nutritional benefit. Before you plump for apples, grapes and bananas – *again*...try apricots, pineapple, pears, nectarines, galia, charentais and honeydew melons, peaches, clementines, oranges, lychees, even sweet ruby grapefruit. All will go down well with kids.

Think of a portion as a handful – using the hand of the child that is going to eat the fruit rather than your own to judge the size of their portion.

Here's an idea for you

Fiddly to eat items will tend to get left, so fill a small pot or freezer bag with peeled clementine segments or fresh pineapple pieces, grapes, sliced strawberries, dried apricots or raisins. Dried fruit does count towards your child's intake of fruit but remember that only one of the portions should be made up of dried fruit – the rest should be fresh.

13. Healthy pre-teens

Find out what your 7–10 year olds need.

- **6–11 servings** of starchy carbohydrates (Bread, potatoes, rice, pasta, breakfast cereals).
  1 serving is: 1 slice bread or ½ cup cooked rice or pasta or ½ cup breakfast cereal or 3 small pieces of potato.
- **3–5 servings** of fruit
  1 serving is: 1 piece fresh fruit or ½ cup tinned or cooked fruit or ½ cup 100% fruit juice.
- **3–5 servings** of vegetables
  1 serving is: ½ a cup of cooked vegetables or a full cup of salad.
- **2–3 servings** of dairy (milk, cheese, yogurts, fromage frais etc)
  1 serving is: a full cup of milk or 1½ pots of yogurt or a matchbox-sized piece of cheese.
- **2–3 servings** of meat, poultry, fish, eggs, pulses, nuts and seeds
  1 serving is: 60–90g meat, poultry or fish or 1–2 eggs or ½ a cup cooked pulses or 30g nuts.

Fatty, sugary and salty foods should be kept to a minimum.

Here's an idea for you

Couscous and chicken salad

This tasty salad makes a change from sandwiches and provides a good mix of carbohydrate, protein, fruit and vegetables. Put 40g dried couscous in a bowl and pour on enough boiling water to just cover it. Cover the bowl with cling film and set to one side for approximately 10 minutes until all the water has been absorbed and the couscous is light and fluffy. Chop up 60g of cooked chicken (leftovers from the Sunday roast will do), a handful of cherry tomatoes, a few dried apricots and a handful of cooked peas and sweetcorn. Stir this into the couscous. If the salad is a little dry add some lemon juice and a little olive oil.

14. The basics

The building blocks of the ideal packed lunch.

A healthy lunch box should contain the following four basic elements. Try to vary the contents from day to day to ensure your child gets a broad spectrum of nutrients.

1. A portion of **protein** such as meat, fish, egg, cheese, beans, lentils, soya products, nuts, seeds or Quorn.
2. Some complex **carbohydrates**. Complex carbohydrates are foods that offer a slower release of energy than refined carbs like white bread, white pasta, biscuits and cakes. Instead use wholegrain, multigrain or granary bread for sandwiches and choose wholemeal pasta and brown rice for salads if possible.
3. A **calcium**-rich food. Cheese, yogurt, yogurt drinks, fromage frais and milk are all good sources of calcium – the mineral essential for healthy bones and teeth. If your child can't tolerate dairy foods, consider alternative sources of calcium such as calcium enriched orange juice and soya milk.
4. At least one portion of **fruit and/or vegetables** for fibre, vitamins and minerals.

Here's an idea for you

Fruit smoothie

Make your own fruit smoothies to provide your children with a hit of fruit and calcium. Hand-held blenders do the job very well and are available cheaply. Take one banana and cut it into chunks. Add five strawberries and ten raspberries. Blend these with three-quarters of a cup of semi-skimmed milk (or calcium-fortified soya milk) or 225ml of natural yogurt until the mixture is smooth. Pour the smoothie into a suitable leakproof container. Most soft fruit works well so why not try mango, pineapple or blackberries. Frozen fruits work just as well and are a more economical purchase. Avoid using flavoured milkshake powders or syrups however, as many are high in sugar and additives.

15. Leave it out

Here's a run down of the worst things you can put in your child's lunch.

- **Ready-made cereal bars, muffins and flapjacks**. They may sound healthy, but they're often high in sugar and fat and come in big portion sizes. Make your own smaller, healthier flapjacks or muffins instead – see opposite, or choose fruit bread, fruit scones or malt loaf.
- **Savoury snack foods.** Over-processed cheese and ham snacks and crisps are usually high in saturated fat and salt. Some savoury snack foods can contain a child's entire daily salt allowance in just one portion.
- **Fruit juice 'drinks' and fizzy pop**. Anything that's labelled as a juice 'drink' is often little more than a fruit flavoured sugary drink – which, like fizzy pop may also contain artificial colourings and preservatives. 100% fruit juice diluted 50:50 with water is a better option – otherwise plain water, low sugar flavoured water, milk or a fruit smoothie.

Here's an idea for you

Banana and date muffins

If you feel like you're taking all the fun out of your child's lunch and want to add a healthier sweet treat, try these. Preheat the oven to 220°C/400°F/gas mark 6. Line a 12 hole muffin tin with paper cases. Beat together 225g/8oz self raising flour, 1tsp baking powder, 110g/4oz light muscovado sugar, 50g/2oz stoned, chopped dates, 3 mashed very ripe bananas, a large egg, 150ml/1/4 pint skimmed milk and 4 tbsps sunflower oil. Pour into muffin cases and bake for 20–25 minutes until cooked through. Cool on a wire rack.

16. Use your loaf

Brown, white, wholemeal, granary, multigrain, pitta or ciabatta – which bread is best for your child?

Bread is a good, nutritious source of complex carbohydrate and vitamins and also contains a beneficial amount of protein.

- **White** bread loses nutrients in processing so has to be fortified with vitamin B1, iron and calcium. Because of this it has twice as much calcium as most other breads.
- **Granary** bread has a nutty taste and good fibre content. One slice has around three-quarters the amount of fibre of wholemeal and an equal iron content.
- **Wholemeal** contains almost three times as much fibre, over three times as much zinc, and almost twice as much iron as white bread.
- **Multigrain** bread has added seeds and wholegrains, which mean it's more slowly digested than many other breads and has a lower glycaemic index, helping to keep energy levels up and satisfy hunger for longer.
- **'Brown'** bread is not the same thing as wholemeal. Most are made from a combination of white and brown flour which means their nutritional content falls somewhere between wholegrain and white bread.

Here's an idea for you

Peanut butter and banana

This tastes good on wholemeal bread or rolls. If your children will only eat jam sandwiches this alternative will give them the sweet hit they're after whilst also providing valuable amounts of protein and a portion of fruit. Peanut butter often has a lot of salt added so try to find a reduced salt or salt-free version (available in health food shops). You don't need to put butter on first, just spread the peanut butter over both halves of the sandwich. Top the sandwich with either mashed or chopped banana.

Hummous and grated carrot

This filling is quite high in fibre so is good for children who will only eat white bread. Just spread hummous (see recipe on page 73) on to white bread or baps and top with one small grated carrot.

17. Weighty issues

If you're worried your child may be overweight read on.

If your child is classed as clinically overweight, it puts him at an increased risk of becoming obese in the future and makes it much more likely he will develop a host of serious diseases such as heart disease, type 2 diabetes, some cancers, arthritis and stroke.

- Encourage your children to recognise when they are full – this may mean that you have to stop encouraging them to finish up everything on their plates.
- Look at the eating habits of the whole family – perhaps there are broader changes you need to make.
- Remember that what you don't buy your child can't eat. Healthy eating begins with the way you fill your shopping trolley.

Never put your child on a diet though, it can lead to eating disorders and image problems later in life. Instead of focusing on the weight issue guide him towards healthy eating. If your child has a healthy, balanced diet, fatty and sugary snacks and drinks are kept to a minimum and he gets plenty of daily exercise, he should maintain a healthy weight.

Here's an idea for you

Satisfying salad

Here's an idea for a healthy salad that will give your child plenty of energy without leaving her feel deprived. The combination of protein foods and high fibre salad will leave children feeling full and provide plenty of slow-release energy to sustain them through i.e. not 'til home time. You will need 30–60g (depending on your child's age) flaked tuna, sliced egg, chopped chicken or tofu, a tomato, a few steamed green beans, cucumber (slice about one inch), grated carrot and some lettuce or other leaf. Combine all the ingredients together. To make a dressing whisk together 2 parts olive oil with 1 part cider vinegar, add a little honey and pour over the salad.

18. Get the right fat-itude

All children need some fat in their diets, but it has to be the right kind.

You need to reduce levels of saturated, hydrogenated and trans- fats and replace them with more unsaturated fats. Here's a guide to what's in what:

- Saturated fats come mainly from animal sources such as butter, lard, hard margarine, red meat, full fat milk and cheese. Coconut oil and palm oil are also high in saturated fat.
- Eating too much saturated fat can increase the amount of cholesterol in the blood, which increases the chance of developing heart and circulatory disease.
- Hydrogenated and trans- fats are found in some biscuits, cakes, pastry, margarine and other processed foods.
- Polyunsaturated and monounsaturated fats come mostly from vegetable sources such as olives, avocados and nuts as well as oily fish and seed, grain and nut oils.

Here's an idea for you

As well as being high in unsaturated fats avocado is one of the richest sources of vitamin E, which is needed for immunity and healthy skin. Avocado also contains some folic acid and a range of other B vitamins. Make this guacamole and include in wraps and sandwiches or as a dip for vegetable sticks. Place 1 ripe avocado (peeled and stone removed), 1 large ripe tomato (deseeded and chopped), ½ a small chopped red onion, a small garlic clove, ½ chopped red pepper and a good squeeze of lemon juice in a blender – and roughly chop – leaving the texture chunky. If you don't have a blender just mash the avocado and mix in all the other ingredients.

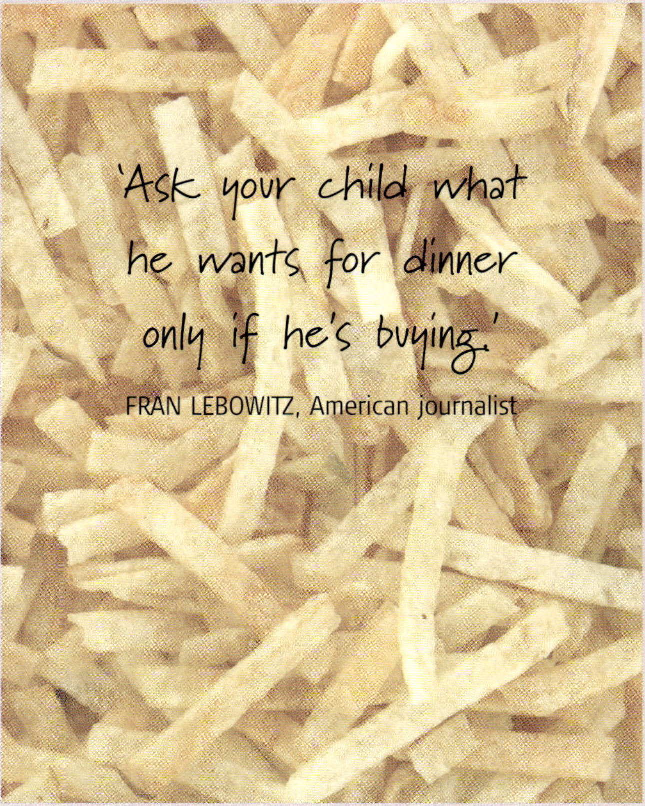

'Ask your child what he wants for dinner only if he's buying.'

FRAN LEBOWITZ, American journalist

19. Chicken little

Chicken can vary enormously in taste and texture, depending on the quality of bird that you buy.

Your average supermarket-bought, factory-farmed chicken will tend to be on the dry, flavourless, fatty side, as birds are often raised with the help of growth promoting hormones then killed relatively early at just 42 days old. This type of bird is also usually farmed indoors, in cramped cages with the help of daily doses of drugs to stave off disease. Free-range, organic chicken on the other hand tends to be more tasty, as birds have to be reared for at least 81 days before they are killed. Growth-promoting drugs are banned and the birds are usually allowed outdoors on a daily basis, with access to grass and freedom to roam.

One of the best ways to serve chicken to children is to give it a bit of extra flavour by marinating it for at least an hour before cooking. Twelve or 24 hours in the marinade is even better (you can also freeze the chicken in these marinades – then take out portions to defrost and cook when you need them).

Here's an idea for you

You can buy pre-flavoured strips of chicken in the supermarket but one look at the bright colour of these products should be enough to tell you that they are full of additives – steer clear. Make your own flavoured chicken instead with one od these marinades:

- 1 tbsp of ketchup, 1 tbsp of runny honey, a crushed garlic clove and 1 tsp of olive oil.
- 1 tbsp of runny honey, 1 tbsp soy sauce, an inch of fresh ginger, grated, (scrape pieces of ginger off the chicken before you cook it) and 1 tsp of olive oil.
- 2 tbsp of natural yogurt and 1 tbsp mango chutney.
- 1 tbsp each of peanut butter and apple juice, 1 tsp of soy sauce and 1 tsp muscovado sugar.

Grill chicken under a medium heat, on a rack over a baking tray – to catch the drips. Try serving it cold wrapped in flatbreads with a little shredded lettuce, tomato and cucumber as part of your child's lunch.

20. Pasta la vista baby

Pasta is a good source of carbohydrate for your children's lunches.

Don't think that you need to make your own pasta or even buy it fresh. On the contrary. In Italy, good quality dried pasta is the order of the day for almost every dish – with the exception of filled pasta like ravioli and tortellini. So keep your store cupboard stocked with a variety of child-pleasing dried pasta shapes and you'll be able to knock up a multitude of popular dishes – for any number of kids – in no time.

Look for farfalle (pasta bows), conchiglie (shells), rotelle (wagon wheels) and, of course, spaghetti and macaroni. For smaller children think fusillini (tiny twists), farfalline (mini bows) and conchigliette (tiny shells) which are now widely available and take just 4–5 minutes to cook. Available from larger supermarkets and some health food stores, Pasta Pals Organic pasta shapes are really worth looking out for as they come in dinosaur, animal and alphabet letter shapes.

Here's an idea for you

Pasta salad

Use your imagination and an appealing pasta shape to create a child-pleasing salad. Tuna, beans (such as kidney, borlotti and pinto) and boiled egg all work well. Add in some chopped tomato and pepper and a handful of peas and sweetcorn. Dress the salad with either some oil and vinegar or *a little* mayonnaise.

21. Fat ideas

Here are a few ideas to help you keep fats at a healthy level.

- Choose lean cuts of meat and trim visible fat.
- Grill, bake, poach or steam rather than frying and roasting.
- If you do choose something high in fat, such as sausages, pick something low fat to go with it – for example, boiled potatoes instead of chips.
- Compare food labels so you can pick the products with less total fat or less saturated fat.
- Swap fatty snacks for healthy ones most of the time, e.g. vegetable sticks instead of crisps, a slice of wholemeal toast with peanut butter rather than cake or biscuits
- Put some extra vegetables, beans or lentils in your casseroles and stews and a bit less red meat.
- Measure oil for cooking with a spoon or use an oil spray rather than pouring it straight from a container.
- Don't use butter or spread in sandwiches if the filling is moist.

Here's an idea for you

Shop bought biscuits and cakes are often high in those bad trans- and hydrogenated fats, so why not make your own instead and get the kids to help? Preheat oven to 180°C/350°F/Gas mark 4. Grease a shallow Victoria sponge tin with a little butter. Put 100g/3½ oz butter, 2 tbsp of golden syrup and 2 tbsp of demerara sugar in a saucepan and melt on a very low heat. Take the pan off the heat and stir in 150g/5oz porridge oats along with a handful of sunflower and pumpkin seeds, which are high in polyunsaturated fats. Tip the mixture into the tin and press down with the back of a spoon. Bake in the centre of the oven for 20 minutes or until until golden brown. Remove tin from the oven and allow to cool for 15 minutes before scoring into wedges. Leave flapjacks in the tin until completely cold.

22. Rice is nice

Kids will love this versatile food.

A delicious, low fat carbohydrate food, packed with vitamins – cooking with rice really can be child's play so don't be put off by it's 'difficult' reputation.

- Basmati is the best rice to use for separate, fluffy grains.
- Use a measuring jug and measure one part rice to two parts liquid. For a child that's roughly 55ml/2fl oz of rice per person to 110ml/4fl oz liquid.
- The best pan to use to cook rice in is a non-stick, wide-bottomed one with a lid.
- Once the boiling liquid has been added, stir once, cover and leave to simmer on the very lowest heat. Do not lift the lid or stir again until the recommended cooking time has elapsed.
- Tilt the pan to see if all the liquid has been absorbed. If it hasn't, give the rice a couple more minutes.
- Remove the lid and cover with a clean tea towel to absorb excess steam. Just before serving, fluff the grains with a fork.

Here's an idea for you

Rice and bean salad

As well as being a good source of carbohydrate, rice contains a useful amount of protein. When combined with beans you get a meal providing all eight of the essential amino acids necessary for health. Rinse half a small can of mixed beans and combine with a serving of brown or white rice and a selection of chopped vegetables such as sweet pepper, cherry tomatoes, sweetcorn, peas, cucumber, salad onions or grated carrot. Throw in a few raisins and pumpkin or sunflower seeds. Dress with a little olive oil and lemon juice or vinegar.

23. Vegging out

Basic nutrition know-how to help if your child's just turned veggie.

If meat is simply left out of main meals and not replaced with a suitable vegetarian alternative, nutritional shortfalls can occur. In particular:

- **Protein.** Beans, nuts, seeds, eggs, soya, cheese and rice are all foods that will add useful protein to a child's vegetarian diet.
- **Iron.** Teenage girls are particularly at risk of iron deficiency, due to blood losses at menstruation. Vegetarian sources include egg yolks, beans, lentils, fortified breakfast cereals, green vegetables and bread. Vitamin C enhances the absorption of iron, so it makes sense to serve fresh fruit or juice with meals.
- **Calcium.** Good vegetarian sources of bone-building calcium include dairy products, fortified soya milk, white or wholemeal bread, green vegetables, tofu, dried fruit and almonds.
- **Zinc.** Zinc is important for immune system function, growth and sexual maturation. Vegetarian souces include cheese, pumpkin seeds, pulses, nuts and tofu.
- **Vitamin B12.** Important in the formation of blood cells and nerves, this vitamin is found mostly in animal foods, but vegetarian sources are dairy products, fortified breakfast cereals and eggs.

Here's an idea for you

Egg and cress.

Why not grow your own cress for this sandwich? Simply moisten some cotton wool or kitchen roll and place on a sunny windowsill and sprinkle with cress seeds. Cress should be ready to eat in 3–5 days. Boil an egg for ten minutes to hardboil it and then immediately cool in a bowl of cold water. Peel and finely chop the egg in a bowl with a small amount of mayonnaise and the cress. Spread the mixture on wholemeal or granary bread to get a filling sandwich containing good levels of protein, iron, calcium and B vitamins.

24. High or low?

How do you know whether a product you're buying is high or low in fat?

To keep an eye on how much fat your family is eating, compare the labels of different food products and choose those with less total fat and less saturated fat. Use the following as a guide:

20g fat or more per 100g is a LOT of fat.
5g saturates or more per 100g is a LOT of saturated fat.

3g–20g fat per 100g is a MODERATE amount of total fat.
1g–5g of saturates per 100g is a MODERATE amount of saturated fat.

3g fat or less per 100g is a LITTLE fat.
1g saturates or less per 100g is a LITTLE saturated fat.

Here's an idea for you

If you're worried that your child is eating too much fat try replacing shop bought biscuits or cakes with this delicious date and walnut loaf. Preheat the oven to 180°C/350°F/Gas mark 4. Grease and line the base of a 1kg (2lb) loaf tin. Chop 225g/8oz dates, add a pinch of bicarbonate of soda and pour over 150ml/¼ pint boiling water. Cream together 75g/3oz butter, 75g/3oz caster sugar and beat in 1 medium egg. Stir in 225g/8oz self raising flour and 75g/3oz chopped walnuts followed by the date mixture. Place mixture evenly in the tin and bake for approximately 1 ¼ hours until firm.

25. Spuds they'll like

A handy, filling food packed with energy-boosting carbohydrates – potatoes are the main ingredient for a host of quick-to-make dishes children will love.

Potato is a starchy carbohydrate food containing some protein, no fat, lots of fibre and a wide range of vitamins including vitamin C. Potato skin is a good source of fibre, and the flesh just under the skin is where most of the vitamin C is stored – so do try to use scrubbed, unpeeled potatoes wherever possible. A portion of new potatoes contains more vitamin C than two fresh apples. They taste great boiled, with their skins on – even when cold.

Store potatoes in a cloth or natural fibre bag somewhere cool, dark and dry. Do not keep them in the fridge (it can cause them to degrade more quickly) and avoid storing them near strongly flavoured foods, such as onions. To cook steam rather than boil and make sure all the pices are evenly sized. Cut your potatoes too small and they will absorb large quantities of water and go slushy – too large, and it'll take ages for them to cook through.

Here's an idea for you

Potato salad

Though not a meal in itself this makes a good extra in a child's lunch box. Scrub clean new potatoes and boil or steam them until just cooked. Once cooked plunge into cold water and leave to cool. When the potatoes are cool cut them into bite-sized pieces and mix in a bowl with some chopped chives, fresh mint or salad onions. Dress the salad with a little mayonnaise or a simple olive oil and vinegar salad dressing.

26. Fishing for compliments

There are shoals of tasty fish varieties out there just waiting to be turned into healthy, child-friendly meals.

Fish is an excellent source of protein, B vitamins, the antioxidant selenium and minerals. Low in saturated fat, oily fish, such as salmon, herrings, mackerel and tuna also has the bonus of being a good source of healthy omega-3 fatty acids, which may help to reduce the risk of heart disease. Fish with edible bones, such as sardines, pilchards and tinned salmon, also contain calcium, phosphorus and fluoride. Calcium is needed for healthy bones, phosphorus is essential for many body functions and fluoride helps to keep teeth strong.

For small children flake all fish really carefully once it's cooked to make sure there are absolutely no bones in it. Buy boned fish and warn older children to look out for stray bones whilst they're eating. The UK Food Standards Agency advise that children under the age of 16 should not eat marlin, swordfish or shark as they may contain higher-than-recommended levels of mercury.

Here's an idea for you

This tasty fish recipe can be used as a dip for vegetable cruditées and breadsticks or as a sandwich filling. Blend 110g/4oz drained can of tuna in spring water or salmon with a garlic clove, 2 tablespoons of olive oil, the juice of a lemon and 2 tablespoons of greek yogurt. Add pepper to taste. Stir in a tablespoon of chopped capers for more sophisticated palates; leave out the garlic if your child does not like the taste.

27. Meaty issues

Red meat has had a bad press over the last few years but don't rule it out of your child's diet. It's a great source of important nutrients.

The best dietary source of easily absorbable iron and an excellent source of protein, B vitamins and other minerals, red meat can also be much lower in saturated fat than you might think. Iron deficiency anaemia is quite common in some groups of young children such as those who are not receiving a good supply of iron from solid foods (other good sources of iron include fortified whole grain cereals and breads, lentils, beans and dried apricots) and those who are given cow's milk as a main drink too early (before 12 months). Iron deficiency can lead to frequent infections, poor weight gain and delay in development.

When buying meat, always look for lean, organic cuts. Trim away excess fat and remove further unwanted fat during cooking: grill chops and steaks and always skim fat from the top of stews, casseroles and meat sauces.

Here's an idea for you

Most processed meat products contain very high levels of salt and additives so it's best to avoid them on a daily basis. If you want to put some red meat in your children's lunch then why not try shredding or thinly slicing leftover Sunday roast lamb or beef and mixing it with some grated carrot, shredded lettuce, sweet pepper, tomato and mayonnaise before putting it in pitta breads, flatbread wraps or rolls. Slices of leftover home made meatballs also work well in this sandwich.

'Ask not what you can do for your country, ask what's for lunch.'
ORSON WELLES

28. Anything with a pulse

Don't dismiss pulses as vegetarian fodder.

There are loads of different varieties of peas, beans and lentils with a wide range of flavours and textures, that can all be used in hundreds of interesting ways. A good source of protein, iron and fibre, beans and lentils can be a vital source of important nutrients for vegetarian children.

Dried pulses store well for long periods if kept in a dry, airtight container away from the light, but it's best to eat them sooner rather than later as they toughen with age and take longer to cook. With the exception of lentils, green and yellow split peas, blackeye and mung beans, most dried pulses need a long soak before they can be cooked, (see pack for directions). Always discard the soaking water, then rinse and cook dried pulses in fresh water without any salt. Salt toughens the skins and makes for longer cooking. Canned pulses, it has to be said, are much, much more convenient (look for salt-free varieties). They're pre-soaked and cooked, so all you have to do is rinse and drain before use.

Here's an idea for you

Hummous

A beige dip made from chick peas does not sound promising – yet a surprising number of kids absolutely adore this Middle Eastern dish. Use it as a dip for vegetable sticks or a sandwich filling. Tahini paste is a sesame seed paste available from health food stores and most large supermarkets.

Throw a tin of drained chickpeas, a crushed garlic clove, 2 tablespoons of tahini paste, 4 tablespoons of olive oil, and the juice of two lemons into a blender and blitz until smooth. Season with a little paprika and black pepper – and sprinkle paprika on top to decorate.

29. Cheese please

Tempt your kids away from those processed, stringy cheese sticks with a little imagination.

From six months of age you can start to introduce a little cheese into your child's diet, either blended into other foods or served in wafer thin slices or tiny cubes. As your child gets older, adding cheese to a dish is almost guaranteed to get him eating absolutely anything – even veggies.

Most types of cheese are an excellent source of calcium – the mineral vital for bone strength and health. Cheese is also a relatively good source of protein, as well as some B vitamins and vitamin A. Eating cheese after a meal has also been shown to help prevent tooth decay – and according to new research, a little cheese before bedtime does not give you nightmares. Its amino acid content can actually help reduce stress and improve sleep.

Aside from these benefits, however, cheese does tend to be high in saturated fat and salt so is always best offered in moderation.

Here's an idea for you

Cheese is a favourite in sandwiches. If you're running out of things to put with it try this coleslaw recipe. Finely chop a few white cabbage or lettuce leaves, grate a carrot and finely slice half a small onion or shallot. Mix together with a little mayonnaise. Other good things to put in a cheese sandwich include grated apple, cooked beetroot or sliced grapes.

30. Egg them on

Eggs are a good source of protein and a brilliant stand-by for a quick, healthy lunch.

A bit of care is needed when buying and cooking with eggs – especially where children are concerned. Follow this guide:

1. At home, always keep eggs in their box, in a cold refrigerator (5°C or below).
2. Wash hands before and after handling eggs to prevent cross contamination.
3 Eat eggs as close to the packing date as possible and certainly within the 'best before date' – use the date on the egg as a guide to freshness. Don't test freshness by putting eggs in a bowl of water.
4. Don't wash eggs since this makes them porous and can let bacteria inside.
5. Do't use cracked or dirty eggs.

Here's an idea for you

Tortilla (serves 4–6)

This tea time treat is also great cold, in packed lunches.

Heat a tablespoon of oil in a medium-sized frying pan, add 2 finely sliced onions and cook over a medium heat until soft. Meanwhile, peel and boil a medium-sized potato until cooked through, drain and then dice into bite-sized pieces. Beat 6 large eggs in a bowl and stir in the onions, diced potato, a small can of sweetcorn, and a handful of frozen peas. Pour the egg mixture back into the still-oily pan and cook over a medium heat for 10–15 minutes until there is no liquid egg left. To flip the tortilla over use a spatula to manoeuvre it onto a large flat plate. Invert the pan over the plate and turn upside down. Cook for another 2 or 3 minutes. Cut into slices to serve.

31. Chocs away

Consistently voted the number one favourite food by children, even the healthiest diet has to find room for a little chocolate now and again.

But did you know that even chocolate has some health benefits? Chocolate is good for you – at least, within reason it is. Chocolate-eating children can enjoy better health than non-chocolate eaters, if they eat the right kind. Dark chocolate with a high (70%) cocoa content is an excellent source of the mineral magnesium and of flavonoids (a special kind of antioxidant) and actually provides more cancer-fighting antioxidants than many fruits and vegetables. *However*, it also provides more calories, so give it to your kids in excess and they'll pile on the pounds. But a few squares two or three times a week will give them an antioxidant boost that will also satisfy a sweet tooth.

Here's an idea for you

White chocolate brownies (makes around 20 brownies)
Preheat your oven to 190°C/375°F/Gas mark 5. Line a 30cm x 20cm/12" x 8" Swiss roll tin or similar with lightly greased aluminium foil. Gently melt 125g/4½ oz good quality white chocolate and 100g/3½ oz unsalted butter in a pan or microwave – then stir in 275g/10oz caster sugar until really well mixed. Add 3 large eggs – one at a time, then 1 tsp vanilla extract and 225g/8oz white chocolate chips. Next stir in thoroughly 175g/6oz self raising flour and a pinch of salt and pour batter into the prepared tin. Bake for 30–35 minutes in the centre of the oven – when done the centre should be only just starting to firm up. Cook them too long and you'll lose the fudgy texture. Allow to cool and set in the tray before turning out, removing foil and slicing into squares.

32. Just desserts

A healthy diet doesn't mean pudding has to be off the menu.

In fact dessert offers a great excuse to add extra fruit and other nutritious foods to your child's diet. Pudding doesn't have to be an everyday event – but it's always handy to have some healthy choices available for those days when your child just wants to eat...and eat.

No matter how nutritious that first course has been, it's best to avoid packet cakes, sweets or chocolate bars for everyday 'afters'. These types of ready-made desserts will all too quickly train your children to expect over-sweetened, artificially flavoured foods – a habit that will be really difficult to break as they get older.

You don't have to be a complete spoilsport however – just make sure junk desserts are the exception rather than the rule. A healthy pud starts at the supermarket, so aim your trolley at the fruit section – if there's no junk in the house – they can't ask for it.

Here's an idea for you

Fruit set in jelly always goes down well and it's super-cheap. Look for packs of real fruit juice jelly, follow the instructions for making it up, then add the fruit of your choice. (Fresh pineapple, kiwi and papaya contain enzymes that will prevent jelly from setting – so are best avoided). Mandarin segments, grapes, raspberries, blueberries and strawberries will all do the trick. Put a few pieces of your chosen fruit in a sealable plastic pot and pour over the jelly mixture. Once the jelly is set, put the lid on and add to your kids' lunch boxes.

33. Whizz it up

Smoothies and shakes really are a great way to bump up your child's daily fruit intake.

Making your own drinks – or allowing the kids to do their own – is really quick and easy too, and a great way to use up excess garden produce or pick-your-own fruit. Overripe fruit, fruit canned in its own juice and frozen fruit also work especially well in smoothies.

Experiment with your own combinations: try to balance tart and sweet fruit, and dense, fibre-rich fruit like bananas, mangoes and pineapple (which also add thickness), with watery fruit such as strawberries, kiwi fruit and oranges.

Even though they are packed with protective antioxidant vitamins and dietary fibre, do be careful how and when you offer these delicious drinks, however. A filling shake or smoothie too close to meal times will dull your child's appetite – and more than one fruit-based drink a day could lead to diarrhoea.

Here's an idea for you

Send your child to school with one of these for break time:

- Rise and shine. This one's high in vitamin C. Blend together a large handful of fresh strawberries, one kiwi fruit (peeled and core removed) and the juice of three oranges.
- Passion fruit and pear refresher. Blend a large, chopped banana, the scooped out flesh from one passion fruit and eight raspberries with the juice from two pears (if you have a juicer) or 150ml real fruit pear juice.
- Tropical treat. Blend together a large banana, the flesh of half a large mango or papaya, the juice of ½ lime and 150ml apple juice.

34. Little chefs

Teaching your children to cook is one of the very best ways to encourage them to adopt healthy eating habits.

Encouraging them to taste as they go will help to make them braver about trying new foods. Cooking teaches planning and organisation, kitchen safety and hygiene. All that weighing and measuring can introduce basic mathematical concepts and creating a dish themselves will nurture their artistic sides.

- Tie back long hair, roll up loose sleeves and wear something that's ok to get messy.
- Wash hands.
- Begin by reading through your chosen recipe from start to finish to make sure you understand exactly what you'll need to do – older children can do this with you.
- Make sure you have all your ingredients and all the necessary equipment to hand before you start.
- Let your child help measure out the ingredients but make sure the ingredients get measured out accurately.
- Observe all the usual kitchen safety rules while you're cooking and never leave a young child alone in the kitchen.
- And finally...make sure they help with the clearing up!

Here's an idea for you

Quick mini quiches (makes 8–12)

Your kids can use a muffin tin to make these portion-sized quiches for lunch boxes. Preheat the oven to 180°C/350°F/Gas mark 4. Roll out a pack of ready-made short crust pastry to a thickness of 3mm. Cut out circles with a 12cm plain cutter and place into the muffin tin. Prick the pastry with a fork, cover with foil and fill with baking beans. Bake for 10 minutes then remove the foil and beans and bake for a further 10 minutes. Remove pastry from oven and turn down to 170°C/325°F/Gas mark 3. Meanwhile, fry a chopped onion and slice a tomato. Whisk together four egg yolks and three whole eggs. Stir in 400ml crème fraîche, 3 tbsp snipped chives and some grated nutmeg. Divide the onion mixture evenly amongst the pastry cases and put a slice of tomato in each, then pour in the egg mixture. Cook for 15–20 minutes until set.

35. Bursting with health

Boost your family's immune systems with the right diet and lifestyle habits to fight off some of the worst infections.

- Make sure everyone is eating a well-balanced diet according to their age and needs.
- Avoid foods that have exceeded their use by dates or seem to be past their prime – they may contain bacteria that can challenge the immune system.
- Lack of sleep leaves us more prone to infection – so put a bedtime routine in place now.
- Stress adversely affects the immune system – so encourage older children to share their worries and learn a few relaxation techniques.
- Regular exercise is important. Apart from boosting circulation and aerobic fitness, regular moderate exercise increases the number of natural killer cells in our body.
- Wash hands frequently and dry with disposable paper towels or freshly laundered towels. Many germs can be transmitted by physical contact. Washing hands frequently can significantly reduce the chances of catching the rotavirus too, which tends to infect children and causes vomiting and diarrhoea.

Here's an idea for you

If your child appears to be coming down with a cold put some of this infection-fighting chicken soup in a flask for her lunch. Bring 2.4 litres/4 pints chicken stock to the boil in a large saucepan. Then add approximately 1.35kg/3lbs lbs rinsed, raw, skinless chicken pieces (ideally, leave the bones in). Return to the boil, turn the heat right down and simmer very, very gently for 1 hour, uncovered. Now slice up the following and add: a large carrot, a large onion, 3 cloves of garlic, a stalk of celery, white and light green parts of a well-washed leek, a parsnip, a peeled sweet potato, a small peeled swede and a handful of fresh dill. Simmer for a further 30 minutes, stirring occasionally. Skim off any fat and season to taste before serving.

36. Supersavers

Feeding your children healthily needn't be expensive if you follow these tips.

- Take some time to roughly plan your meals for the week and then make a shopping list. Keep paper and a pencil in the kitchen, so you can write down items as you think of them.
- 'Buy one, get one free' and three for two offers are only good value if they are for products you would buy anyway.
- Learn the tricks of the trade. Well-known brands pay a premium to have their goods displayed at eye level. The cheaper brands will usually be hiding on the lower levels.
- The prices really are better when you buy in bulk – but watch out for the pitfalls. Concentrate non-perishable items (such as canned goods) or those with a distant 'best before' date.
- Seasonal fruit and veg will always be cheaper than the 'just flown in from Kenya' sort. Adapt your cooking to accommodate seasonal foods and think about buying fresh produce from local markets rather than supermarkets. It will almost always be cheaper.

Here's an idea for you

Use seasonal English apples to make this great dip or sandwich filling for children with a sweet tooth – especially those who refuse to have anything but jam sandwiches. Blend together a 250g pack of soft, low fat cream cheese, 3 tablespoons of low fat mayonnaise, a tablespoon of lemon juice and 2 peeled and chopped apples. Add chopped walnuts for more sophisticated children or an adult version of this dip.

'An apple is an
excellent thing –
until you have tried
a peach.'
GEORGE DU MAURIER,
illustrator and novelist

37. Save more

Here are some more tips on keeping the weekly food bill down.

- Sign up for a supermarket loyalty card – you'll be paid points for a certain percentage of your spending.
- If you're not going to the supermarket for a major shop, take a basket or small trolley at the door. It's harder then, to overload with unnecessary items.
- It's much cheaper to eat foods made from scratch than prepared foods.
- Next time you cook – whether it be lasagne, soup or cake double the amount, then freeze half of it.
- The highest-cost item on many people's shopping lists is meat. Start cooking one or two vegetarian meals every week, use non-meat fillings in sandwiches and make salads with beans, cheese or eggs instead – it's a healthier and cheaper way of eating.

Here's an idea for you

If your kids are always clamouring for the expensive packets of cheese strings, dippers and biscuits try these snack suggestions instead:

- small cheese chunks and sliced apple or pear
- dried fruit and unsalted nut mixes – try a selection from chopped, dried apricots, dates, raisins, cashews, peanuts, almonds, sunflower seeds and pumpkin seeds. Get children to make up their own selections.
- oatcakes, rice cakes or breadsticks

38. Salt solutions

How can you minimise the amount of salt your children eat?

- Check the labels on processed foods so you can choose those with the least added salt or sodium.
- Don't add salt to your cooking.
- Don't put salt on the table.
- Cut down on salty snacks such as crisps and nuts, and heavily salted foods such as processed meats, cheese, pickles and smoked fish.
- Choose tinned vegetables and pulses that say 'no added salt'.
- Cut down on sauces, especially soy sauce, because these are usually very high in salt.
- Ask for unsalted chips and fries in restaurants and burger bars.

Here's an idea for you

Add flavour to foods with herbs and spices and you'll find your children need less salt in their meals or could even do without! Fresh herbs will generally give the best results but it's good to keep a selection of dried herbs in the cupboard too.

- Basil is great in salads, especially when combined with mozarella and tomato.
- Chives have a mild onion flavour and are great to add flavour to egg sandwiches, cream and cottage cheeses and salads.
- Parsley is a great source of vitamin C and the B vitamins. Use the flat or curly variety and add to salads, soups, couscous and rice.
- Cinnamon is a brilliant spice for adding flavour to fruit, cakes and biscuits.

39. The big freeze

If you make a few lunchbox favourites and keep them in the freezer you won't spend all of your evenings making up packed lunches.

- Only freeze food that it is really fresh and in good condition.
- Never put foods that are still slightly warm into the freezer.
- Pack and seal food with care using freezable containers or freezer bags.
- Freeze food in single or double portions. It freezes faster, takes less time to thaw and allows you to defrost the exact quantities you need.
- Never re-freeze food once it has thawed.
- Never let food thaw in a warm environment – instead let it thaw out slowly in the fridge.

Where possible, use square and rectangular containers to store food in the freezer – they stack better and waste less space. Alternatively, pre-form liquids (or solids with liquids, such as stews) in square blocks by pouring the liquid into a polythene bag which is sat inside a square-sided container. Freeze it like this, then remove the solid block from the container and seal the bag.

Here's an idea for you

Spinach and feta cheese triangles

Make a batch of these tasty and healthy mini-pies and freeze them for your children's lunches. Unlike other pastries, filo contains no fat; spinach is rich in iron and calcium. Preheat oven to 200°C/400°F/Gas mark 6. Wilt the contents of a 400g packet of fresh spinach in a large pan (you only need to add a spoon or two of water). Once the spinach is cooked leave to cool before squeezing all the excess moisture out and chopping finely. Crumble a block of feta into a bowl and combine with the spinach, a beaten egg and a little melted butter or oil. Take a sheet of filo pastry and cut in half lengthways. Spoon a small amount of spinach mixture near the top of the first strip and then fold the opposite corner over to form a triangle shape. Continue folding corner to edge until you have used all the pastry strip and have a triangular parcel; brush with a little butter. Bake for 10–15 minutes until golden brown.

40. Big kids

How to encourage hungry teens to eat nutritious meals.

Growth and development are especially rapid now, so the need for energy and certain nutrients is particularly high. This demand differs significantly between boys and girls. Boys need quite a bit more protein and energy at this age than girls due to their greater growth spurt.

Ideally, teenagers should be eating:

- At least five portions of fruit and veg a day.
- Carbohydrates (e.g. bread, pasta, rice, potatoes) with every meal.
- Several servings of milk and dairy products daily.
- One or two servings of protein (meat, fish, eggs, nuts and pulses) each day. Include at least two portions of fish a week – one of which should be an oily fish.
- Only small, limited amounts of fat, including butter, margarine, oils and cream, and fried foods including crisps and chips and small, limited amounts of sugary foods including cakes, biscuits, sweets, soft drinks, and ice cream.

Here's an idea for you

Healthy 'between meal' snacks that your teen can take to school include:

- fruit of any kind – sliced, dried or tinned in juice;
- cold lean meats in a wholegrain bread sandwich;
- peanut butter on rice or oatcakes;
- hummous or cream cheese dips with bread sticks, chopped vegetables or fruit;
- fruit milkshakes made with semi skimmed milk or a fruit smoothie;
- a pot of yoghurt;
- home made snack mixes of dried fruits, nuts and seeds with a handful of chocolate chips, mini pretzels or mini marshmallows thrown in. Divide the mix into individual portions in re-sealable plastic bags.

41. Calcium is key

All children need an adequate intake of calcium, to help with bone and dental health.

Teenagers need particularly high amounts and the rapid increase in bone mass at this time of life means that teenagers actually require more calcium than adults. Boys should aim for 1000mg calcium per day and girls 800mg. A well balanced diet that includes a pint of milk a day should give enough calcium to fulfil these requirements.

Other good sources of calcium include dairy products such as yogurt and cheese (low fat milk and dairy products contain at least as much calcium as whole milk and its products), calcium-fortified soya milk and white bread. Pulses, nuts, dried fruit and green vegetables, such as spring greens and broccoli also contain calcium, as does fish that is eaten with the bones, such as whitebait or canned sardines.

Here's an idea for you

Salmon and watercress sandwich

Canned salmon is a good source of calcium since it contains the fish bones. These are very soft so simply mash them up with the rest of the fish. The dark green leaves of watercress also contain plenty of calcium. Mash the salmon up, with a little cider vinegar and ground black pepper if desired, and garnish with the watercress. Serve on wholemeal or fortified white bread or rolls.

If you also include a natural or flavoured yogurt and a handful of dried fruit and nuts in your child's lunchpack he will be well on his way to reaching his daily calcium requirement.

42. Iron out deficiencies

Make sure your kids aren't missing out on this essential mineral.

All children require a good intake of iron, particularly important in the formation of haemoglobin, which transports oxygen round the body in the blood. Adolescents have been shown to be at particular risk of iron deficiency. In one national survey almost 50 per cent of teenage girls, as well as a significant proportion of boys, were found to have a low intake of iron. Rapid growth, coupled with poor dietary choices, can result in iron-deficiency or anaemia – which can lead to chronic fatigue, heart palpitations and affect academic performance. Teenage girls need to pay particular attention to iron in their diets as their iron stores are depleted each month following menstruation.

The main dietary source of iron is red meat, but there are lots of non-meat sources too, including fortified breakfast cereals, dried fruit, bread and green leafy vegetables. The body doesn't absorb iron quite as easily from non-meat sources, but you can enhance absorption by combining them with a vitamin C rich food like orange juice and fresh fruit and vegetables.

Here's an idea for you

Pack your kids' lunches with iron by chosing some of the following every day:

- Fortified lunch products – many large supermarkets now have ranges especially catering for the nutrient needs of school-age children.
- A selection of dried fruits, or a cereal bar containing dried fruits.
- A carton of juice to aid absorption of iron from non-meat products.
- Fruit and vegetables to aid absorption. Broccoli is a good source of both iron and vitamin C and can be eaten raw with hummus or cream cheese dips.
- Bread, wholewheat pasta or brown rice.

43. I think I'm going to be sick

The good news is, many children do eventually go on to outgrow their food allergies and intolerances.

The most common food allergies and intolerances are cow's milk, egg, nuts, wheat gluten, fish, shellfish, citrus fruits, tomatoes, sesame seeds and soya.

A true food allergy will usually cause an immediate reaction after eating a particular food. Symptoms can occur a few seconds or minutes after eating. The most common symptoms are itchy skin, itchy or swelling tongue and lips, sneezing, blocked or runny nose, shortness of breath and coughing. At its severest allergy can lead to anaphylaxis, which is life-threatening.

A food intolerance gives a much more delayed reaction, often occurring hours or even days after eating certain foods. It will often involve digestive problems of some kind. Symptoms may include tummy pain or colic, bloating, wind, diarrhoea, and sometimes vomiting. A food intolerance can cause a lot of discomfort and over time, malnutrition, but it is not immediately life-threatening.

Here's an idea for you

If an allergy or intolerance is diagnosed, you will probably have to become an expert at reading food labels. Your child's lunches will take a lot more planning but with the wide choice of specialist foods available these days, and a greater public awareness of allergy and intolerance it doesn't have to be a nightmare. Make sure that your child's school knows what he is allergic to and let all the other children know. Children are curious and like to swap foods so make sure everyone knows what foods he cannot eat and ensure that your child knows that he must not eat anything other than what you have sent him to school with.

44. Snack attack

Make sure what they eat for morning break is healthy too.

Snacking itself isn't necessarily a bad thing. Young children frequently need one or two snacks a day as their stomachs are so small they simply can't get all the nutrients and calories they need through meals alone. For children of all ages, the right snacks can also help to keep blood sugar and energy levels up and can even improve their concentration levels throughout the day.

It's the content of your child's snack that makes all the difference, however. Pre-packaged snack foods such as crisps, biscuits, processed cheese and cakes tend to be high in calories, salt, sugar and additives – and low in nutrients. These fattening, energy-sapping foods are best avoided.

Bananas are a great snack and the Banana Guard solves the problem of bruised and battered fruit. A handy plastic case that fits most bananas, it also gives kids somewhere to store that smelly, sticky skin until they get home. Available in 9 funky colours (including glow-in-the-dark), log on to www.bananaguards.co.uk or call 01473 211138 to order.

Here's an idea for you

If your child has refused breakfast, you will probably need to provide a more substantial snack for elevenses that will fill a hole but won't spoil her appetite for lunch. Good suggestions include:

- Vegetable crudités with hummous;
- Fromage frais with berries or fruit puree;
- Oatcake and a slice of cheese;
- Fruit and yogurt smoothie;
- Slice of malt loaf or fruit loaf;
- Pieces of apple and a handful of nuts.

45. Fruit machine

Hit the jackpot with these exciting alternatives to apples, pears and bananas.

Take your pick from the fruit below:

- Berries. High in vitamin C and fibre and delicious stirred into yogurt, added to fruit salad or thrown into a fruit smoothie.
- Mangoes. With one of the highest levels of antioxidant nutrients, beta carotene and vitamin C mango is delicious pureed and added to yogurt and fromage frais or simply cubed and served on its own.
- Kiwis have a higher vitamin C content than oranges. Cut the kiwis in half before wrapping them in plastic wrap. Best eaten with a teaspoon, like a boiled egg.
- Plums and prunes. Prunes are very sweet and a good source of blood-boosting iron, and both have good levels of fibre. Be careful to control the amount your child eats however as both fruits have well known laxative properties.
- Watermelon. Super sweet watermelon is high in antioxidants and a rich source of potassium, which helps keep the body's fluid balance in good order. Pick out the pips, and serve in chunks or blend the flesh and drink as a smoothie.

Here's an idea for you

In the summer taking children to a local a pick-your-own farm will encourage them to eat fruit. Kids will really enjoy a Sunday afternoon spent picking – and, of course, eating – strawberries, raspberries, plums or blackberries. Alternatively, get your child to grow her own fruit – even if you don't have a garden. Strawberries and tomatoes (yes, the latter are, of course, fruit) do really well in pots, window boxes and gro-bags and are easy to look after. You can buy starter plants very cheaply from all garden centres at the beginning of the summer.

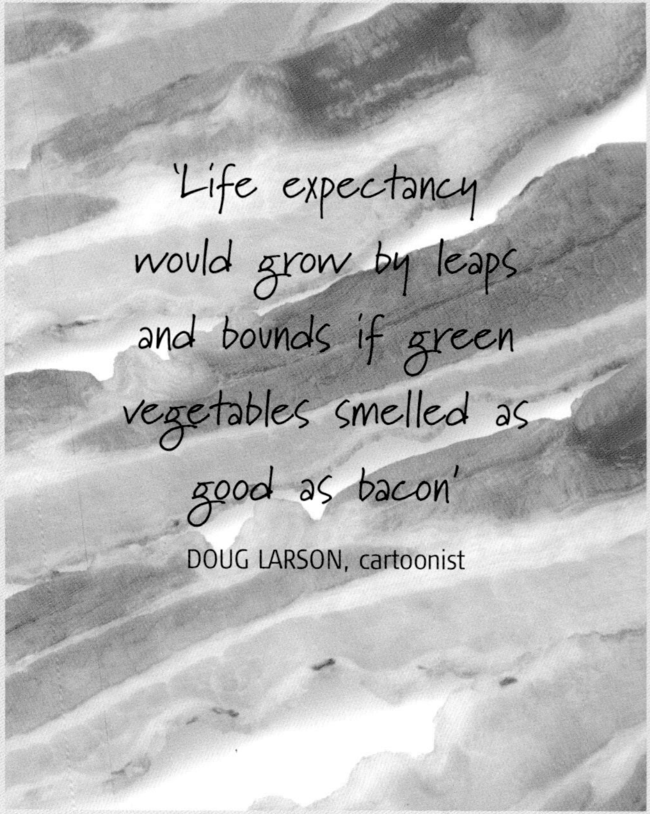

'Life expectancy would grow by leaps and bounds if green vegetables smelled as good as bacon'

DOUG LARSON, cartoonist

46. Start right

Many schools run breakfast clubs – and if you drop your child off early in the morning for one of these you'll need to provide something substantial for him to eat.

A well-balanced breakfast can have a noticeable impact on your child's health, mood, ability to concentrate and eating habits for the rest of the day. Some studies have also found strong links between eating breakfast and improved learning. Eating the right foods at breakfast time will stabilise blood sugar levels, making it less likely that your child will crave a boost from sugary, high fat or processed foods later in the day.

The foods to avoid at breakfast are the sugary and over processed ones which tend to lead to cravings for yet more sugary, over processed foods by midmorning. So avoid foods like chocolate, pastries or honey-coated and sugar-frosted cereals. Instead, try to ensure your child has a combination of slow-releasing carbohydrates and protein, which will help to keep him full and offer a steady supply of energy until lunchtime, along with some fruit.

Here's an idea for you

Try these packed breakfast ideas:

- A wholegrain cereal (with minimal added sugar and fat – compare labels to find the best) served with chopped banana and semi skimmed milk. Put the cereal and banana in separate pots and the milk in a carton or bottle so the breakfast doesn't go soggy on the way to school.
- Wholegrain, multigrain, seeded or fruit bread with low sugar and salt peanut or other nut butter, reduced-sugar jam, a thin spread of butter and Marmite (use Marmite sparingly as it is high in salt), mashed banana or cream cheese. Serve with some fruit juice or fruit slices on the side.
- A pot of natural bio-yogurt with fruit and muesli stirred in. Tempt reluctant kids to try this by letting them choose their own additions.

47. Sugar, sugar

Whilst the odd bag of sweets will not do any harm it's important to cut down on your family's everyday consumption of sugar.

Some foods that you might not expect to have sugar added to them can contain lots, for example some 'healthy' breakfast cereals and cereal bars. Other foods can be higher in added sugar than you might expect, such as tins of spaghetti or baked beans. The only way to really find out is to read the labels.

When you are checking food labels look for the 'carbohydrates (of which sugars)' figure in the nutrition information panel on the label.
10g sugars or more per 100g is A LOT of sugar
2g–10g sugars per 100g is a moderate amount of sugar.
2g sugars or less per 100g is A LITTLE sugar

The higher up the ingredients list sugar is, the more sugar the product contains. Be aware that small amounts of lots of different sugars such as sucrose, glucose, glucose syrup, golden syrup, maple syrup, treacle, invert sugar, hydrolysed starch, honey, dextrose and maltose may be added. Add them all up, and sugar may outweigh anything else in the recipe.

Here's an idea for you

- Have fewer sugary drinks: go for water or unsweetened fruit juice instead.
- Instead of cakes or biscuits, try a currant bun, a slice of melon or some malt loaf.
- Do not add sugar to hot drinks or breakfast cereal.
- Rather than spreading jam on sandwiches, try peanut butter, reduced sugar jams, mashed banana, or low-fat cream cheese.
- Choose tins of fruit in juice rather than syrup.
- Watch out for things like reduced fat salad dressings which often have more sugar than the full-fat version
- Check food labels to help you pick the foods with the least added sugar or go for the low-sugar version.

48. A big problem?

What to do if you think your child is overweight.

If you have concerns about your child's weight before doing anything else you must seek advice from your GP. Your child's nutritional requirements will fluctuate with age, so don't be tempted to cut foods or groups of foods out of her diet unless you have been advised to do so by a doctor or registered dietician. Around the onset of puberty girls and boys suddenly need many more calories to fuel the dramatic changes their bodies are going through. Girls start to deposit extra fat on their breasts, hips and thighs and boys become taller and more muscular. These developments are normal – so it's important they are not mistaken for weight problems.

Give your child plenty of encouragement and positive feedback – whatever her size. If your child is overweight, don't start to obsess about it. Eat meals together and set a good example with your eating habits. Frequent weigh-ins, nagging and singling her out for special diet meals can just lead to more problems and may even encourage an eating disorder.

Here's an idea for you

Panzanella is a nutritious and unusual Italian salad and a brilliant way to use up stale bread – get your child to tear up the bread and help with the chopping! Break a thick slice of stale ciabatta or similar open-textured bread into bite-sized pieces. Place in a bowl with 1–2 ripe tomatoes cut into chunks, some finely chopped red onion, some cucumber cut into pieces the same size as the tomato, a finely sliced stick of celery, a teaspoon of pesto, 1 tbsp olive oil and freshly ground black pepper. Stir well and leave for 30 minutes. Add some protein such as half a can of fish, a little cheese or a hard-boiled egg to make a hearty lunch.

49. Plan-it organic

The best food you can buy for your family – or just a big con?

Organic farming methods are designed to maximise the health of the environment and animals on the farm. The use of artificial fertilisers, herbicides and pesticides is severely restricted and animals are reared without the routine use of drugs, antibiotics and wormers that are more common in intensive livestock farming. Genetically modified (GM) crops and ingredients are currently banned under organic standards. The result is produce that contains the absolute minimum of chemical residues and has a lower environmental impact than conventionally farmed foods.

To be able to call itself organic, a food or drink must have been certified organic by an independent body like the Soil Association. In the UK organic standards are rigourous. For a product to mention the word 'Organic' in its name at least 95% of its ingredients must be organic, and the label must tell you which ingredients are not. The non-organic ingredients can only be used because there are no organic versions of them.

Here's an idea for you

These are the best organic things to try in your kids' lunches:
Fruit and vegetables – you'll avoid worries about pesticide residues and tests have shown that on average organic fruit and veg contains higher levels of vitamin C, essential minerals and antioxidants than its conventional cousins.
Fruit squash – colours, stabilisers and preservatives which have been linked to hyperactivity and artificial sweeteners which may pose a particular risk to young children are not allowed in organic versions. But be warned, it's still high in sugar.
Dried fruit – as well as being produced from organic fruit, preserving ingredients such as sulphur dioxide, which can cause wheezing in sensitive individuals, are not allowed in organic dried fruit.
Dairy produce – organic milk and cheese can contain almost 75% more of the essential fatty acid omega 3.*Wholemeal bread* – high-fibre bread is the most likely type of bread to contain pesticide residues because they can collect in the grain's outer layers – so buying organic does make sense.

50. Eat fat

When is fat good for your kids?

Up to the age of 5 a child's diet should contain around 40% fat; after that it is suggested 30–35% of their calories should come from fat. Whilst no child should be put on a low fat diet unless advised by a medical expert to do so, there is substantial evidence that reducing the amount of 'bad' saturated, trans- and hydrogenated fats we eat can lower the chances of becoming obese or developing conditions such as heart disease, type 2 diabetes and some cancers. These unhealthy fats should be replaced with reasonable levels of healthy unsaturated fats.

Many experts now believe that the balance of omega 6 (found in plant oils) and omega 3 fatty acids in children's diets may be crucial for health. The bulk of children's polyunsaturated fat intake currently comes in the form of omega 6s – so many experts believe it's the level of omega 3s, found in oily fish like mackerel and salmon that needs to be improved. Children who have taken part in trials of fish oil supplements appear to have better concentration, learning ability and behaviour – but more research is needed. Eating oily fish regularly can help to reduce the risk of coronary heart disease.

Here's an idea for you

If your kids hate fish here's a way of getting the omega 3 fats into them without resorting to supplementation. Columbus Omega-3 rich eggs are sold in most large supermarkets and come from chickens that are fed on omega 3 polyunsaturated fatty acid-enriched feed. Hardboil the eggs and add to salads and sandwiches, try tortillas (page 77) or mini-quiches (page 85) or make an omelette and chop up pieces into a pasta or rice salad.

51. Happy shoppers

Healthy eating starts with the shopping trip.

To challenge your child's tastebuds, take her shopping with you and encourage her to choose one 'new' food item that's not on the regular list to take home and try every week. If she's a timid eater, start off with something really simple – like letting her choose a new pasta shape, breakfast cereal or dessert. If she's a little braver, fruit doesn't have to mean bananas and grapes. Lychees kumquats, star fruit, cape gooseberries, pomegranates, guava, custard apple, passion fruit and papaya can all be found in large supermarkets at different times of the year. Let your child choose an unusual fruit to be shared by the family for dessert.

All kids love sausages, so try swapping your regular chipolatas for one of the more interesting varieties flavoured with sundried tomatoes, garlic or cranberry. Again – allow her to decide which it's to be. Take a look at the herbs and spices. Let your child pick the most interesting one she can find and then work a recipe around it later in the week.

Here's an idea for you

If it seems impossible to get your child interested in fruit meet her half way with these sweet dips for fruit slices.

- Greek yogurt. A pot of half fat Greek yogurt, fromage frais or creme fraiche with a swirl of fruit puree, lemon curd or honey and chopped toasted almonds.
- Caramel dip. Super sweet, but great with bananas slices and apple cubes – simmer a large, unopened can of condensed milk in a saucepan of water over a low heat for 1 hour (the water should be half way up the can – so check and top up water levels). Remove the can from the pan extremely carefully and leave to cool for at last 20 minutes before opening – to reveal a delicious toffee-coloured caramel.

52. Petits gourmets

Challenge your child's palate with some unusual foods and flavours.

One theory is that children pick up their tastes for various foods in their mother's womb and through the different flavours that permeate breast milk. So perhaps one of the keys to raising an unfussy eater is to eat a varied diet – including plenty of the foods you want her to eat once she's older – whilst you're pregnant and breast feeding.

Once a child is 12 months old and can eat more widely, don't be afraid to offer her new tastes. Many of us are guilty of serving nothing but 'safe', bland meals, because we're afraid anything too unusual may simply be rejected. Remember, the broader her diet, the more likely she is to be getting all the nutrients she needs. Most children are naturally cautious about foods, so always offer one new food at a time and in small quantities. Approach anything new with the attitude that you're giving her something delicious to try rather than timidly handing it over and waiting for her to turn up her nose. You may well be surprised by what she will accept and enjoy.

Here's an idea for you

Beansprouts are a superfood that more adventurous children will love to grow and eat. Sprouts are young green plants germinated from the seeds of vegetables, nuts, grains or beans and they've got antioxidants in super-concentrated amounts. Buy some mung beans from the supermarket or health food shop; rinse, then soak in clean water for 12 hours. Rinse again, and pour the beans into a clean glass container. Cover the container with clingfilm to stop the beans drying out – and place on a cool, bright window ledge. Rinse the beans and replace in the container every morning and every evening (this is important to avoid mould formation). Within 4–5 days your beans should have started to germinate. Your crop is ready to eat when most of your sprouts have developed two small leaves. Beansprouts can form part of your children's lunches as a snack, in sandwiches or in salads.

brilliant ideas

This book is published by Infinite Ideas, creators of the acclaimed **52 Brilliant Ideas series**. If you found this book helpful, there are other titles in the **Brilliant Little Ideas** series which you may also find of interest.

- **Be incredibly creative:** 52 brilliant little ideas to hone your mind
- **Catwalk looks:** 52 brilliant little ideas to look gorgeous always
- **Drop a dress size:** 52 brilliant little ideas to lose weight and stay slim
- **Find your dream job:** 52 brilliant little ideas for total career happiness
- **Heal your troubled mind:** 52 brilliant little ideas for tackling stress and defeating depression
- **Healthy children's lunches:** 52 brilliant little ideas for junk-free meals kids will love
- **Incredible sex:** 52 brilliant little ideas to take you all the way
- **Make your money work:** 52 brilliant little ideas for rescuing your finances
- **Perfect romance:** 52 brilliant little ideas for finding and keeping a lover
- **Raising young children:** 52 brilliant little ideas for parenting under 5s
- **Relax:** 52 brilliant little ideas to chill out
- **Shape up your bum:** 52 brilliant little ideas for maximising your gluteus

For more detailed information on these books and others published by Infinite Ideas please visit www.infideas.com.

See reverse for order form.

Qty	*Title*	*RRP*
	Be incredibly creative	£5.99
	Catwalk looks	£5.99
	Drop a dress size	£5.99
	Find your dream job	£5.99
	Heal your troubled mind	£5.99
	Healthy children's lunches	£5.99
	Incredible sex	£5.99
	Make your money work	£5.99
	Perfect romance	£5.99
	Raising young children	£5.99
	Relax	£5.99
	Shape up your bum	£5.99
	Add £2.49 postage per delivery address	
	Final TOTAL	

Name: ....

Delivery address: ....

....

....

E-mail:.............................Tel (in case of problems):............................

By post Fill in all relevant details, cut out or copy this page and send along with a cheque made payable to Infinite Ideas. Send to: *Brilliant Little Ideas*, Infinite Ideas, 36 St Giles, Oxford OX1 3LD. **Credit card orders over the telephone** Call +44 (0) 1865 514 888. Lines are open 9am to 5pm Monday to Friday.

Please note that no payment will be processed until your order has been dispatched. Goods are dispatched through Royal Mail within 14 working days, when in stock. We never forward personal details on to third parties or bombard you with junk mail. The prices quoted are for UK and RoI residents only. If you are outside these areas please contact us for postage and packing rates. Any questions or comments please contact us on 01865 514 888 or email info@infideas.com.